For President Will—

Alvin Silverstein
Virginia Silverstein

BIONICS

Other books by the Silversteins

BIONICS

Man Copies Nature's Machines

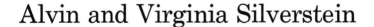

Alvin and Virginia Silverstein

Illustrated by Penelope Naylor

The McCall Publishing Company
New York

FOR **Ruth** AND **Aaron Colish**

Copyright © 1970 by Alvin and Virginia Silverstein
Illustrations copyright © 1970 by Penelope Naylor

ALL RIGHTS RESERVED.
Published simultaneously in Canada by
Doubleday Canada Ltd., Toronto
Library of Congress Catalog Card Number: 74–117017
SBN8415-2013-5
FIRST PRINTING
PRINTED IN THE UNITED STATES OF AMERICA

The McCall Publishing Company
230 Park Avenue, New York, New York 10017

Contents

BIONICS

What Is Bionics?

In total darkness a bat can snare an insect without ever having seen it. It follows each dodge and turn of its prey. The bat accomplishes this amazing feat by sending out high-pitched sounds that bounce off objects in its path. When the sounds bounce back, the bat's keen ears pick them up. Its brain analyzes the sound signals to tell the size and shape and speed of these objects. Sometimes the bat is out-maneuvered. Certain moths, for instance, have very keen "ears" of their own. They can pick up the bat's signals, and they twist and turn and dive out of its range.

In these two animals nature has created remarkable sound detecting and analyzing systems. They are millions of times smaller and far more sensitive than any man has ever made. It is not surprising, then, that scientists and engineers are busily studying bats and moths to learn how their sound-detecting systems work. Indeed, in laboratories throughout the world, scientists are studying all sorts of animal systems to discover the answers that nature has worked out to problems that man, too, would like to solve.

Animal eyes are providing clues for the construction of better television cameras and air traffic control systems. The sonar or sound-location systems of bats and dolphins are being used as models for improving man-made location systems. Senses of touch and smell and heat detection are being studied in many different animals in hopes of finding ways to apply them to man's needs.

Leopard frog with model of electronic eye.

The mysteries of animal migration and the amazing time-keepers that animals have built in are being explored. These studies may someday lead to better instruments for navigating not only on earth but in travels to other planets as well.

Studies of how dolphins swim effortlessly through the water and birds glide through the air have already helped engineers to build better ships and airplanes.

Among the strangest sights in nature are living things that give off their own light. These lights are fantastically efficient, and if man can learn to duplicate them his cities may be brighter at a much lower cost. The electric eel and other animals that can produce and store large amounts of electricity also hold valuable secrets to unlock.

Of all the studies of living creatures, perhaps the most important and far-reaching are those of how the brain thinks and remembers and learns. We are just at the beginning in our efforts to build machines that can really think. As we learn more about nature's thinking machines, we may be able to build true robots and supercomputers that will work with man to help solve the problems of our world.

The study of systems in living creatures and their applications for the improvement of man-made systems form the science of *bionics*. This is a new science. Even the name "bionics" was not made up until 1960. But this infant science has grown spectacularly. Already it has brought in valuable results, and it promises much more for the future.

Machines That See

Most of what we humans know about the world around us is brought to us through our sense of sight. With our eyes we receive a constant flow of information about the size and shape of objects, their color and texture, how near or far they are, and whether they are moving or standing still. Nearly every action normally involves our sense of sight, and we are so used to relying on our eyes that we may not realize just how amazing the process of vision really is.

When you reach out to catch a ball and then quickly send it flying back again, your eyes have reported a flood of information about the size, shape, and position of the ball and of the other players. Your brain, like a superfast computer, has put all this information together to figure out exactly where the ball will be at each instant of time.

Scientists and engineers would very much like to learn how to devise machines that can "see." Such machines would have many uses. Computers could work much faster and more effectively if they could "read" the letters on a printed page instead of having to have human beings carefully translate each word into an electrical machine language. Scanning machines could aid in guiding the swarms of airplanes circling above an airport, could help to bring spaceships in for safe landings on strange planets, and could even guide automobiles safely through a maze of rush-hour traffic. Much progress has been made, and simple seeing machines have been devised. The area of sight is one that is being eagerly studied, and bionics has already contributed some important practical results.

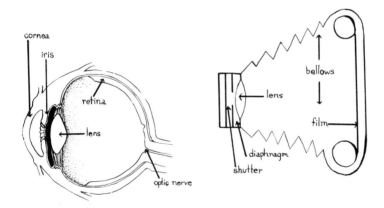

A simple camera works very much like a human eye.

It is often said that a camera works very much like the human eye. In a camera, a lens focuses rays of light onto the film, where special light-sensitive chemicals react. The exposed area can then be developed with other chemicals to form an image or photograph of the scene that the camera "saw." In the eye, the focusing lens is not glass but a structure of living tissue, filled with a watery fluid. The light rays are focused onto a light-sensitive layer at the back of the eyeball, called the retina. Unlike the chemicals in camera film, which can be used only once, the light-sensitive cells of the retina can react over and over again, forming a continual series of patterns that are sent to the brain through messages that travel along the optic nerve. In the brain these are translated into meaningful images, and so it is really with our brains that we "see," rather than just with our eyes.

In fact, the brain is able to make some amazing adjustments in interpreting the messages sent by the eyes, in order to work out the finely detailed pictures that we see. In some experiments at Innsbruck University in Austria, researchers tried wearing distorting spectacles that made images seem blurred, with straight lines curved and the angles all out of proportion. They wore these glasses all the time, and strangely, after a week or so, the distortions seemed to fade away and everything looked normal again. Then, when they took the glasses off, the world seemed distorted once more, and it was some days before their brains relearned to see things properly.

Although the brain's part in seeing is vitally important, there is some evidence that the eyes themselves do part of the job of sorting out which details are important and which are not. There are about a hundred million tiny sense cells in the retina of a human eye, and only about a million nerve fibers leading from the eye to the brain. Experiments in which special instruments followed the movement of people's eyes as they watched a luminous dot moving on a screen have shown that the eyes are able to track the movement of the dot and even figure out in advance where it will go next. All this is done in a split second—in a far shorter time than would be needed to send messages to the brain and back again.

There are many difficult problems in studying the human eye. First of all, it is enormously complicated—one of the most complicated seeing machines in the whole animal kingdom. Moreover, the human eye does not stay still, as a camera does. It is constantly moving, back and forth and about, in such tiny rapid movements that you probably would not be able to notice them even if you stared at yourself in a mirror. By this constant shifting, the eyes are able to focus clearly on different parts of a scene in quick succession, constantly adding new details to the picture that the brain pieces together. Then too, the kinds of experiments that a researcher can do with human eyes are very limited. He cannot do anything that will harm the eye or result in a loss of vision. He cannot cut certain nerves to see what will happen, or even implant tiny electrodes. For all these reasons, scientists have turned to experiments with animals to find simpler and more convenient models to study.

The frog's eye, which contains nearly five million cells, may not seem terribly simple. But it does not move about constantly as the human eye does; instead it may remain fixed on one spot even when the frog turns its head. And for various other reasons the frog's eye has proved to be a very useful model for the study of sight.

Researchers at the Massachusetts Institute of Technology, headed by Jerome Lettvin, have done some important work with the common leopard frog, *Rana pipiens*. They have found that the frog's eyes bring it a picture of the world very different from the one we see. The frog's picture is a much simpler one, but it is enough for his needs. In order to survive, a frog has to be able to catch his food and keep from being caught by swooping birds or pouncing animals. A frog eats insects, which he catches with lightning flicks of his long tongue. Therefore, the only details that are really important to a frog are moving things: small, insect-shaped objects moving toward him, which he can catch; large, threatening objects moving toward him, which might catch him; and

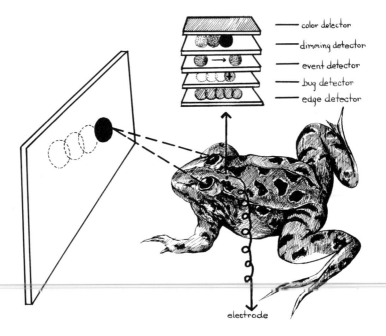

color detector

dimming detector

event detector

bug detector

edge detector

electrode

The picture that a frog sees is built up from the signals from five different kinds of detectors.

menacing shadows overhead, which might mean the approach of a bird. With these types of information a frog can react quickly. If an insect is flying toward him, he can follow its flight and catch it when it comes into range of his tongue. If a threat is looming near, he leaps—hopefully into the water, but if he hits the ground he can always try leaping again. He does not need to be able to see clearly blades of grass or trees or rocks, or anything else that does not move; these details are not important in his world.

The scientists at M.I.T. showed frogs objects on a screen; tiny electrodes carried messages from fibers of the optic nerve and thus indicated when the frog was actually seeing things. It was discovered that the frog's eye contains five different kinds of cells, each contributing a different kind of message, which together make up the frog's picture of the world. "Edge detectors" pick up the outlines of things, provided that they are moving and have a shape that might be "interesting." For example, the frogs did not respond to a motionless circle or square, or to a moving square, but a rapid fire of messages traveled along the optic nerve whenever a circle was made to move. The second type of cells was labeled "bug detectors." These sense cells work to sharpen the outline and pinpoint the exact location of the moving object. "Event detectors" pick up the sensation of movement, and "dimming detectors" signal a sudden darkening that might mean a threatening shadow. Finally, the frog's eyes contain "color detectors," which are sensitive to only one color—a watery blue. These sense cells help the frog to jump toward water, where he would have the best chance to escape from danger.

At the Radio Corporation of America, scientists built a very simple electronic model of a frog's eye. It contained 1,600 light detectors and was mounted on a board forty inches square. This electronic eye was able to see simple objects and to pick out the patterns of fly-shaped objects from other shapes. Because the frog's eye is designed to detect *moving* objects, electronic systems based upon it can have important applications. They can be used to keep track of airplanes circling above an airport and thus feed information to computer-run air traffic control systems. They can be used in warning and defense systems that provide protection from attack by enemy missiles. And such electronic eyes will be needed if we are ever to have automatically guided automobiles. For the task of a driver is in some ways very much like the problems of a frog sitting on a lily pad. He must have a constant flow of information about objects moving toward him—cars, signposts, pedestrians crossing the road. But there are many other distracting details that are not important at all—cars on the other side of the road, billboards, an argument between the children in the back seat. All these details might cause a human driver to take his attention away from his driving, but a robot driver with froglike electronic eyes would not notice them at all.

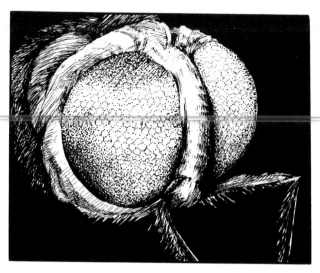

The eye of a common housefly is made up of thousands of tiny lenses.

In addition to the frog's eye, nature has come up with a totally different plan, which is also quite effective for detecting moving objects. This is the compound eye, possessed by many insects and various other animals. Our eye, and that of the frog, has just a single lens. But an insect's compound eye is made up of many tiny lenses, each of which focuses light onto a specialized sense cell. Some ants that live underground have compound eyes made up of only six of these parts, or ommatidia. The housefly's eye has 4,000 ommatidia, while the dragonfly's eye has 28,000 tiny lenses. Each ommatidium registers a picture of a small part of the insect's environment. All these parts fit together like the tiny

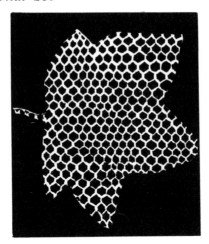

Mosaic-like picture from an insect's compound eye.

colored tiles of a mosaic. The more ommatidia, the more detailed the picture—so it is not surprising that the dragonfly is one of the keenest-eyed of all insects.

Compound eyes generally do not give as clear a picture of the world as our type of eye, but they are wonderfully suited for detecting and following movement. As an object moves across an insect's field of vision, it passes by first one ommatidium and then another and another in succession. Messages are flashed to the insect's brain, and the picture that it receives is like a series of tiny lights flashing on and off across a board. This kind of vision is very useful to a dragonfly trying to catch a fast-flying mosquito, and it is equally helpful to the mosquito trying to escape. It would also have useful applications in man's world.

One interesting series of studies of compound eyes has been conducted not on insects but on the horseshoe crab, *Limulus*. This creature is really not a crab at all, but a rather primitive animal related to the spiders and scorpions. Its body is encased in a horseshoe-shaped suit of armor, and it crawls along the sea bottom. The horseshoe crab's compound

The horseshoe crab has a simpler type of compound eye.

eye is made up of about 1,000 ommatidia. H. K. Hartline of the Rockefeller University, who has studied the creature, has discovered that the response of one ommatidium to light is affected by the ommatidia around it. If just one ommatidium is stimulated, it sends a rapid fire of messages along the optic nerve fiber, which can be picked up by tiny electrodes. But if a nearby ommatidium is also stimulated, it seems to inhibit the response of its neighbors. Then neither of the stimulated sense cells sends as strong a message to the horseshoe crab's brain. Hartline discovered that a network of branching fibers not only connects the sense cells with the brain but also connects neighboring ommatidia with one another. This effect makes contrasts seem sharper and helps the horseshoe crab to see clearer outlines.

At the General Electric Company, David Hildebrand built a seeing machine that was a simple model of the horseshoe crab's eye. In this electronic model, each light detector was linked with the two photocells next to it. This principle is now being used to design a device that will help in making television images clearer.

The study of another compound eye has already brought some important practical benefits. At the Max Planck Institute in Germany, it was discovered that the beetle *Chlorophanus viridis* measures its flight speed by the time it takes for an object to move from one part of its compound eye to another. This gave the United States Air Force engineers an idea: they mounted photocells in the noses and tails of airplanes and linked them up with a computer. This produced a highly reliable ground speed indicator for airplanes.

Machines That Hear

Sounds are becoming more and more important in our world. Nearly all man's machines make noise, from tapping typewriters to humming automobile engines. And when many machines run at the same time, they can add up to quite a loud noise. The sharp *rat-a-tat-tat* of a pneumatic drill or the whine of an electric saw can shatter the quiet of a neighborhood. Some modern music is so loud that doctors now fear that it may hurt the ears of people who listen to it. Even a "silent" electric clock makes a whirring sound that we can hear easily when other sounds are absent.

Many scientists are studying noises and ways of making them quieter. The are also studying how we and other members of the animal kingdom hear, and they have already developed some interesting applications for man-made systems.

The outer part of the ear acts as a sound-gathering device.

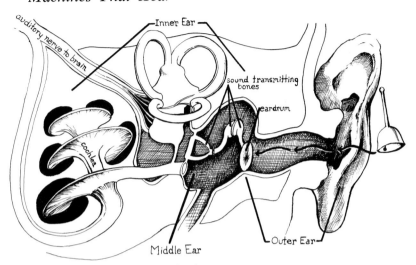

The human ear.

Our ears are not very effective sound funnels, but dogs, horses, and many other animals can prick their ears up and turn them about to act as efficient antennae. At the entrance to the ear is a thin membrane, the eardrum. This vibrates like the top of a drum when sound waves push against it. The sound vibrations pass along a series of three small bones and then to another membrane, which covers the opening to a fluid-filled chamber. Within this chamber, which is coiled like a snail shell, the fluid vibrates, too, and presses on special hair-tipped sense cells, which send messages to the brain. There the vibrations are sorted out and we hear them as sounds.

We get a surprising amount of information from sounds. Sounds can be high or low, loud or soft. From these qualities we can often figure out what is making the sounds and how near or far it is. Since we have two ears, one on each side of the head, we can compare the loudness of the sound that each ear hears and so figure out the direction from which it is coming. Of course we do not usually think about all these things consciously; our brain does the figuring automatically.

We also have a curious ability to listen *selectively*. We can follow the voice of a friend while we carry on a conversation in a crowded room, mentally screening out all the noise in the background and concentrating only on what we want to hear. A mother can pick out the sound of her own child's voice among all the other sounds of the neighborhood, and she will even wake from a sound sleep if she hears her baby crying, although a loud clap of thunder may not make her stir at all. And if a noise, even a fairly loud one, goes on for a long time and we do not consider it important, our ears can automatically "turn off" so that we are no longer aware of it at all.

All these abilities of human ears are of interest to the bionics specialist. They are studying how we hear in an effort to devise machines that can hear and interpret human speech. Already a simple model of an electronic hearing machine has been developed. It picks up human speech and transcribes it on a typewriter. It does not have a very large vocabulary, but it is a beginning.

But human ears are not the best models for studying hearing. Nature has many sound experts who have far keener ears than we do. Dogs, for example, can hear sounds much higher pitched than those that human ears can hear. A "silent" dog whistle makes a noise up in this very high-pitched range, which scientists call "ultrasound." Rats and mice can also hear sounds in the ultrasonic range, and they can make ultrasounds too. They use them to communicate with each other. Cats have equally keen hearing, and they can tune in on rodent conversations, which help them to locate their prey.

A great variety of animals can make and hear sounds, and use them to communicate with one another. Among the noisiest of earth's creatures are the birds, which have special songs to establish a territory or win a mate or warn of danger. Studies of bird language have even brought some practical benefits. In one town that was plagued by starlings nesting thickly on the roofs and in trees, a researcher had an ingenious idea for getting rid of the pests. He recorded the starling's distress cry and then played back the recording through an amplifier. The frightened starlings, convinced that there must be some extraordinary danger nearby, took wing and flew away.

By far the best hearing specialists of all land animals are the bats. These night hunters can hear far into the ultrasonic range and use their acute hearing to catch their prey. The whir of a mosquito's wings or the rustle of an insect crawling on a leaf is enough to give it away to a sharp-eared bat. But

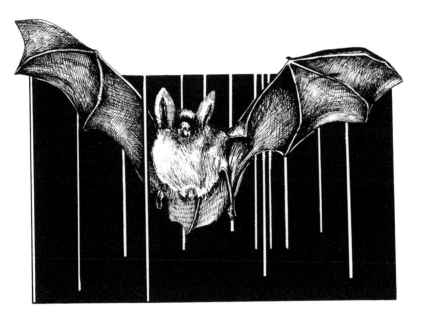

A bat finds its prey by sending out high-pitched sounds and analyzing the way they bounce back.

many moths are equipped with effective muffling devices, such as rows of fine hairs along the edges of their wings, which smooth their flight and allow them to fly noiselessly. Yet the bats are able to catch these moths too, even when it is too dark to see them. Bats can also fly about their crowded caves in pitch darkness, without bumping into one another. Curious scientists began to test bats in the laboratory. They found that a bat can fly easily through a darkened room in which dangling wires a fiftieth of an inch wide hang from the ceiling only a wingspan apart—and the bats do not even brush against the wires. In total darkness, a bat can not only catch mealworms thrown up into the air, but it can also tell whether its "prey" is a mealworm or only a small stick of the same size.

If a bat is blindfolded, it can still find its way about perfectly well. But if its ears are plugged or its nose or mouth is taped up, it blunders about helplessly, bumping into things. Sound recording and high-speed motion picture photography have helped to solve the mystery of how bats find their way around so well. They use a sort of sound-location, or sonar, system. Through its nose or mouth, the bat sends out a series of very high-pitched sounds—ultrasounds. If there is anything in the bat's path, the sound waves bounce and return as echoes. The bat's large ears funnel in the re-turning sound echoes and send messages to its brain. The part of the bat's brain that deals with analyzing sounds is larger and better developed than any other part of its brain. It is like an efficient computer center, whose job is to put to-gether the patterns of the echoes and from them figure out what kind of object they bounced off, how far away it is, and how it is moving. So efficient is the bat's brain that it can not only locate prey as tiny as a mosquito but can plot a flight path to intercept it. A researcher has recently built an electronic model of the bat's brain and the link with its sonar

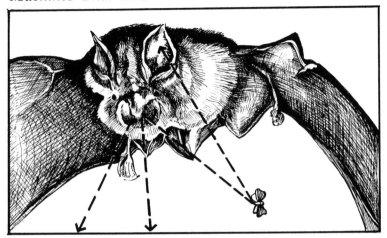

A bat can easily find its way through a maze even when blindfolded.

system, and he has actually reconstructed three-dimensional pictures of objects that the bat "sees" with its ears.

Even more amazing, in a way, than the bat's sonar system is the way the moth uses its hearing apparatus to defend itself. The bat, after all, is a rather intelligent animal, with a highly developed brain and a very efficient pair of ears. The moth's ears are two tiny structures on the sides of its body, each consisting of only a small "eardrum," an air sac, and two nerve cells running to the moth's tiny brain. When the moth picks up the bat's ultrasonic cries, it reacts immediately. Some moths merely fold up their wings and drop to the ground. This is not a completely effective defense, however, because although the moth has suddenly changed course, its fall to the ground follows a predictable path. With a little experience with this kind of moth, a bat soon learns how to compute the path and can catch many insects that try this trick.

But some moths try a more complicated maneuver. They immediately change course and dart away from the bat, even flying straight upward if necessary. It seems that even with their simple ears and brain they are able to determine almost instantly just where the bat is.

Some night-flying moths have an even stranger defense against bats: they make ultrasounds of their own. When the bat hears these special moth cries, it immediately flies off and does not bother the moth any more. Scientists were at first puzzled by this behavior. For their experiments had shown that bats' sonar is not bothered by any other sounds —records of bat cries, loud blasts of wide-ranging noise. Then they discovered that most of the moths that make such sounds are very bad-tasting. If a bat catches one by mistake, it immediately spits it out. And so the ultrasonic moth cries seem to be interpreted as warning cries.

The bat's sonar is very similar to the radio location (radar) and sound location (sonar) systems that are now used to help ships and planes navigate, to map the ocean bottom, and in a growing number of other applications. But

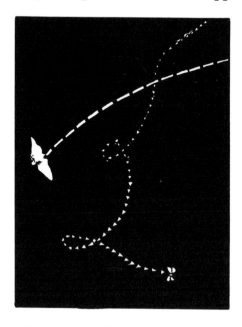

A moth dodges and dives to escape from a bat.

in perfecting man-made sonar systems, researchers have also made good use of another sonar expert, the dolphin.

For a long time it was thought that the world of the sea is a silent world. But when underwater microphones were devised, researchers discovered a continual chorus of clicks and whistles, cackles, grunts, and roars. Many different kinds of fish have been found to communicate with each other by sound. They send out mating calls and call to one another to keep their schools in order, threaten rivals, and warn of danger. Amid this chorus of fish sounds, the sea mammals—dolphins, whales, sea lions—communicate with their own kind and navigate through the water, avoiding obstacles and locating their prey with a sonar system very much like that of the bats. Since water conducts sounds better than air does, dolphin sonar works very effectively indeed. In one experiment, blindfolded dolphins easily retrieved a bag of pebbles from a deep pool, with only their sound location system to guide them. Studies of dolphin sonar are still being actively pursued, even though we now have workable radar and sonar systems of our own. For dolphin sonar is far more compact and efficient than any electronic sonar system that man has yet been able to devise.

Curiously, man himself has been found in recent studies to have some ability for sonar. Usually we do not develop this ability very much; we rely mainly on our eyes. But blind people often use a variety of sounds, such as hisses and tongue clicks, to help them find their way about. They can learn to tell the size and shape of objects, and even to distinguish finer differences, such as different kinds of cloth. In one experiment, blind people were found to be able to sense the presence of a target only an inch and three quarters wide at a distance of twenty-four inches, and a ten-inch target nine feet away, using their own sonar. Perhaps electronic amplifiers and analyzers will one day help blind people to "see" their way with the aid of sound.

Other Senses

A male silkworm moth emerges from its cocoon and for a time remains motionless, resting. Then suddenly he is in the air, flying furiously upwind. The breeze has brought him a faint scent—so faint that we could not smell it at all; perhaps there are only a few molecules of the scent chemical. On the moth flies, until at last he has reached his destination several miles away: a female of the species. There they mate.

The secret of the male silkworm moth's fantastic sense of smell lies in the two feathery antennae that sprout from the front of his head. They contain many thousands of sense cells, which respond to just a single chemical, the scent chemical produced by female silkworm moths that are ready to mate. Even after the male has smelled the special odor that tells him that the female is somewhere about—at least within a few miles of him—how does he find her? Does he

*A male silkworm moth smells with his sensitive
antennae.*

follow the scent, seeking ever stronger and stronger traces
of it? That is the way a hunting dog follows a trail and a bee
finds its way to a familiar flower. But the scent that lures a
male silkworm moth to his mate is often so faint that he
would have to fly a great distance before it would get any
stronger. Scientists are still not completely sure how the
moth solves his problem, but it seems likely that the scent
just prompts him to fly up into the air. Then another unusual
sense comes into play: a wind direction indicator in the
joints of his antennae. Once he has determined the wind
direction, instinct prompts him to fly upwind, toward the
source of the breeze that brought the scent. And eventually
he finds his mate.

The animal world is filled with senses that we either do
not possess or barely use, for we rely mainly upon our sight
and our hearing. Many animals, from insects to lions, have
keen senses of smell and use odors to help find and win a
mate. Each species has its own special sex attractant—an
odor that the female (or perhaps the male) sends out to

attract others of its species. Researchers have succeeded in finding out how some of these odor chemicals are put together and have made some of them in the laboratory. Now sex attractants look like promising weapons in the fight against insect pests: only the insects of a particular species are attracted to a trap or poison by their own special sex attractant, and helpful insects and other animals are not affected at all. Animals often use scents for other purposes as well, to mark food trails or to mark off chemical "no trespassing" signs around borders of their territory. Fish and other water animals use a similar chemical sense, taste, to communicate with each other. Tastes in the water carry mating signals and tell young barnacles where the colony has settled down. It is believed that salmon find their way back to their birthplace to spawn by the particular tastes of the water.

Scientists are fascinated by these chemical senses in the animal world. They can think of many applications for an "artificial nose"—if they could only devise one. Such an invention could be used to analyze mixtures of chemicals in the food and chemical industries and in many others. Crime detection would be revolutionized—a few sniffs at the scene of the crime, and then the criminal could be positively identified when he was arrested. An artificial nose could be useful in medicine, for doctors believe that a sick person's body makes many unusual chemicals, which could be used to diagnose his illness quickly.

So far man's best attempt at an artificial nose has been the gas chromatograph, in which a mixture of substances is turned into vapors, which are separated as they flow along in a stream of gas. The gas chromatograph can be used to detect quite small amounts of substances—perhaps one part in a million parts of other substances. But a dog or a moth can do much better than that, in a much shorter time, and

A rattlesnake finds its prey by sensing heat. It will even strike at a warm lightbulb.

with much more compact apparatus. Even humans, with their weak sense of smell, can pick up many faint scents to which the best gas chromatographs are completely "blind." So it seems that man still has some way to go before he can match the efficiency of nature's chemical detectors.

In other senses, too, members of the animal world have achieved a degree of efficiency that man would love to match.

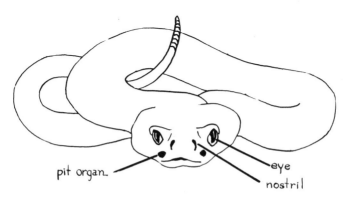

A rattlesnake showing the heat-sensitive pit organ.

Many insects, for example, have an extraordinary sense of touch. Through the nerve endings in its legs a cockroach can detect a movement of 1/254,000,000 of an inch! A rattlesnake can find its prey with ease even if its eyes are taped. It still "sees" the world through another organ, a small pit between its eyes filled with heat-sensitive cells. These sense cells are very similar to the ones with which we tell whether objects are warm or cold. We have only about three such cells on each square centimeter of skin, while the rattlesnake's pit organ contains about 150,000 of them in the same area. With this heat sensor the snake can tell the difference between two objects whose temperatures are only a thousandth of a degree apart. This unusual sense organ helps it to find the warm bodies of its prey. Human inventors have used a similar principle in devising antimissile weapons such as the Sidewinder, which homes in on a source of heat.

In addition to heat sensors that can distinguish fine temperature differences, some animals seem to have a feeling for absolute temperatures, without any need for comparison. Bees keep an even temperature in their hive, all year round, by an amazing sort of community air-conditioning system. When the weather is cold they crowd together around the breeding cells, conserving their body heat and keeping their young warm. On hot summer days they bring water into the hive and fan their wings to make it evaporate, sending the hot, damp air out through the entrance of the hive. In some termite mounds in Africa, a complicated system of tunnels and air vents in the mound helps to circulate and cool the air within. Termite workers toil tirelessly, opening and closing vents and widening and narrowing tunnels, so that the temperature within the queen's chamber will stay just right.

One of the oddest "living thermometers" is the incubator bird, a brush turkey of Australia. This bird hatches its eggs

The Australian incubator bird tests her mound to make sure the eggs are at the proper temperature.

in a mound of leaves and grasses. For six months the mother bird stays by the mound, continually taking samples with her beak and testing the temperature. If the decaying vegetation and the heat of the sun are making things too hot, she digs air vents to cool the mound. At night, or on cloudy days, she covers the mound with an insulating layer of sand to keep the heat in. Somehow she manages to keep her eggs at just the right incubator temperature of about ninety-one degrees.

With heat and chemical detectors, as well as even stranger detectors of gravity, magnetic fields, electricity, and perhaps others of which we do not yet know, the world of animal senses holds many secrets that human inventors are eager to learn and apply.

Nature's Clocks and
Compasses

Have you ever awakened just before the alarm clock rings in the morning? Many people do. And some can even decide, before they go to sleep at night, just what time they are going to wake up the next morning—and then wake within a minute or two of that time. It seems that the body has an inner clock of some sort, which runs automatically and never needs winding.

Scientists have discovered many such clocks in the living world. Single-celled creatures living in a drop of pond water have them, and so do plants and animals of various kinds. Some plants lift their leaves up during the day and fold them down at night. The fiddler crabs that run about at the edge of the sea change color each day, darkening during the daytime and turning pale at night. Some of the inner clocks seem to be set to a timing cycle of approximately twenty-four hours. These are called *circadian* rhythms, from Latin words

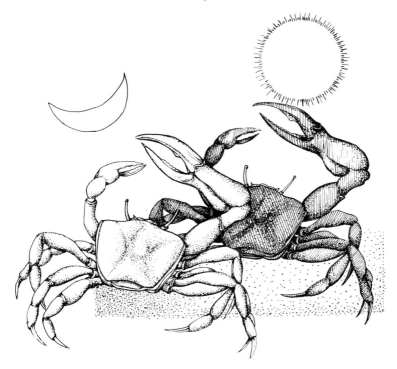

The fiddler crab changes color according to the time of day.

meaning "about a day." Other biological clocks are timed to the ebb and flow of the tides, or the phases of the moon, or the seasons of the year.

At first, scientists thought that these accurately timed cycles were reset each day by the rising and setting of the sun, or the flow of the tides, or other influences of the out-side environment. But then it was discovered that plants in a darkened laboratory still go through their daily cycle of "sleep movements" even though the rays of the sun do not reach them. Fiddler crabs in quiet laboratory tanks, away from both sunlight and the wash of the tides, still carry on their daily cycles of activity and rest and color changes just as though they were in their normal homes. Even animals bred in the laboratory through many generations show the same kinds of rhythms that their ancestors did.

Sometimes biological clocks can be reset. If you were to fly from New York to London, where the time is six hours later, you might feel upset for a day or two. When everybody else was sleepy, you would be wide awake, and you would feel sleepy at your old, New York bedtime. But soon your body would adjust, and you would be in tune with your new neighbors. Scientists have taken advantage of the ability of biological clocks to be reset in order to study more conveniently the habits of animals that are active at night. They simply put the animals in laboratory rooms without windows and set the lights to go on at night and off during the day.

For example, for a long time very little was known about the mating habits of guinea pigs, even though these are among the most common of laboratory animals. This peculiar situation was due to the fact that guinea pigs usually mate in the middle of the night, when scientists are home asleep. A researcher solved the problem by resetting his guinea pigs' inner clocks. After a few weeks of living on an artificial nighttime "day" and daytime "night," the guinea pigs began to be widest awake just at the time when the scientists were working in the laboratory and could study them easily.

Researchers are still not entirely sure just how nature's inner clocks work. Hormones, chemicals that help to control the body's activities, seem to be involved in many cases. Some experiments seem to indicate that periodic changes in the earth's magnetic field or in the pressure of the air may be factors that set biological clocks. Pieces of potato, for example, were found to be very sensitive to tiny changes in the air pressure and could even be used as a sort of biological barometer to predict changes in the weather. It is hoped that the experiences of astronauts, who leave the influences of the earth behind, and experiments with animals and plants sent out into space, will bring more information about these strange rhythms of nature.

Scientists are interested in biological clocks not only for their own sake but also for their connection with an even more intriguing problem: the amazing ability of many animals to navigate. Many species of birds, turtles, fish, seals and whales, and even insects are noted for their long migrations, often over vast expanses of open sea where there are no landmarks to guide them. Amazingly they are able to trace the same routes year after year. Even the young of the group, if held back until their experienced parents have already left on their migration, are somehow able to find their way.

Studies of animal navigators have revealed some incredible stories. Green turtles regularly travel 1,200 miles through open sea from their feeding areas off the coast of Brazil to their breeding grounds on lonely Ascension Island. Fur seals return from the sea each year to mate on the barren Pribilof Islands of Alaska. So perfect is their timing and navigating skill that the females usually land within a day of when they are ready to give birth to their pups. Twice a year naturalists eagerly chart the migrations of the whooping cranes from their winter nests in Texas to their summer breeding grounds in Canada and back again. The ability of homing pigeons to find their way back to their cages is well known. But perhaps the record in this department is held by the Laysan albatross. When the United States Navy built an air base on one of the Midway Islands in the Pacific, they found that albatrosses nesting on the island were interfering with the flights of the planes. They did not want to kill the birds, so they decided to try to resettle them somewhere else. As a test they flew eighteen albatrosses to various places along the Pacific coasts—the state of Washington, Alaska, Japan, New

Guinea, and Samoa. Within a few weeks, fourteen of the birds were back again at Midway.

Researchers have found that migrating animals use a variety of inner compasses to help them navigate. Some steer by the position of the sun. Others navigate by the stars. Some use the sun as their guide during the day, and then switch to star navigation by night. One study shows that the homing pigeon uses the earth's magnetic fields as a guide in finding its way home, and there are indications that various other animals, from insects to mollusks, can also make use of magnetic compasses. It is of course very useful for a migrating bird to be able to switch to a magnetic compass

A scout bee reports to the other workers in the hive with a "tail-wagging dance."

when clouds cover the sun; otherwise he would just have to land and wait for the sun to come out again.

Even with the sun or stars to steer by, the problems of navigation are more complicated than they might seem at first. For example, a worker honeybee that has found a rich source of nectar and pollen flies rapidly home to the hive to report. A German naturalist, Karl von Frisch, has discovered that the bee scout delivers her report through a complicated dance in the hive, in which she tells the other workers not only how far away the food is, but also what direction to fly in relation to the sun. But the sun does not stay in one place all day. As the workers start out to gather the food, the sun may already have changed its position in the sky somewhat. In later trips during the day, the sun will seem to move farther and farther toward the west. Yet the worker bees seem to have no trouble at all in finding the food source. Their inner clocks tell them just where the sun will be, and they change their course correspondingly. These amazing inner clocks even tell the bees what time to start out in the morning on their first foraging trip of the

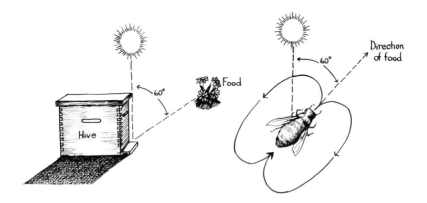

The worker bees find food by navigating according to the position of the sun.

day and what time to stop work so that they will not be caught in the dark on their way back to the hive. They are able to figure this out even though the days change their length according to the seasons of the year.

In addition to determining the position of the sun and consulting its inner clock, the foraging honeybee has a further problem of navigation. The bee is so small that even a slight breeze will tend to blow her off course. But the bee can solve this problem too. Special wind-speed indicators in the joints of her antennae give her air speed, while a glance at the ground below, through her two compound eyes, gives her ground speed. Automatically her brain uses this information to work out the angle she has to hold against the wind to reach her destination.

Nature's amazing navigators have evolved their skills over millions of years. Now human scientists are eagerly studying biological clocks and compasses in search of ideas for new navigating systems for man, which may someday take him not only across the face of the earth, but even out into deepest space.

Nature's Mechanics

Since the first simple machines, such as the lever and the wheel, were invented, man has been building devices to increase the efficiency and power of his own strength. As new sources of power have become available, especially in the last century or two, machines have become capable of accomplishing tasks far beyond the strength of any living thing. Engines are often rated in "horsepower," and it may give an automobile owner pride to realize how many horses it would take to equal the pulling power of his car's engine.

But now, as we strive to make our machines ever more powerful and efficient, scientists are belatedly realizing that nature has some valuable lessons for us. Muscles—the muscles in our own arms and legs, for example—are amazingly efficient machines that convert chemical energy directly into mechanical energy (motion). Man-made engines, from the engine in an automobile to a great turbine, generally convert fuel (chemical energy) first into heat or electricity, and only then is this energy converted into mechanical energy. But with each step along the way, some energy is lost. And thus the muscle, with its one-step conversion, is far more efficient than an automobile engine or a turbine.

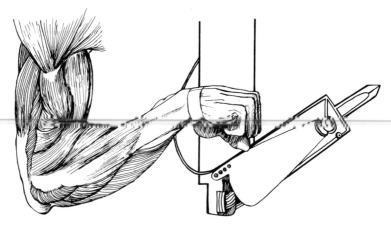

Some mechanical arms are modeled after the human arm.

Scientists are now trying to devise musclelike machines that could convert chemical energy directly into motion. Just how does a muscle do this? It contracts, and in doing so exerts a force that can pull up a weight or do other useful work. One researcher placed a fiber of collagen, a protein substance that is found in skin and other living materials, inside a long tube, fastening one end securely. The other end of the collagen fiber was attached to a wire, which passed over a pulley. A weight could be hung on the end of the wire. When the tube was filled with a strong salt solution, the collagen fiber immediately contracted, pulled on the wire, and pulled up the weight. When the salt solution in the tube was replaced with water, the fiber relaxed again, and the weight was lowered. The researcher then made the machine automatic, by hooking up the wire to a set of valves that opened and closed as the fiber contracted or relaxed, alternately filling the tube with salt solution or water. Other researchers have built similar artificial muscles from a synthetic polymer fiber, polyacrylic acid.

A slightly different approach to the building of artificial muscles is through the use of inflatable tubes that contract as they are filled with air or compressed gas, and thus can be made to do work. Such a "muscle," expanded by carbon dioxide from a small storage tank, has been used to power artificial hands for amputees. Artificial-muscle engines may also find use in control mechanisms for hydraulic valves and in other industrial applications.

As man increasingly explores areas where he himself cannot safely venture, he is more and more copying nature's mechanisms in devising manipulators to work for him. The discovery of radioactivity and the use of radioisotopes has spurred on such research. For although radioactive materials are finding more and more uses each year, they are extremely dangerous to handle. Even thick, lead-lined gloves do not provide enough protection in many cases, and humans can work safely only behind many feet of shielding. There they watch through special windows as mechanical manipulators do the work for them. The operator moves the control levers, and metal fingers pick up and measure and transfer the radioactive materials.

Such mechanical manipulators can perform enormous feats of strength that would not be possible for a man. They can also be made to perform amazingly delicate tasks. For example, Japanese researchers at Nagoya University have devised a set of mechanical manipulators for use inside germfree chambers. In this case there would be no danger for humans inside the chambers; instead, the danger would be that germs from the human workers would contaminate the animals that are kept inside under absolutely sterile

A mechanical manipulator in a germfree chamber can perform very delicate tasks.

conditions. The metal fingers of the manipulators can be moved with such fine precision that they can be used to feed and care for small experimental animals such as mice and rats, picking them up and even giving them injections without hurting them at all.

Researchers at the General Electric Company, in a project sponsored by the United States Army, have been developing a "pedipulator"—a walking machine. This is a vehicle that will stride along on twelve-foot legs, at perhaps thirty-five miles an hour. It will be able to cover rough terrain where vehicles with wheels or even caterpillar tractors could never go at all. It should be useful in rescue work and in exploring dangerous areas. And, of course, one of the

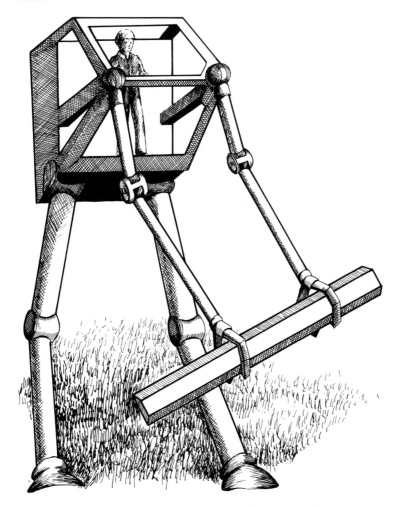

A pedipulator is designed for heavy jobs and rough terrain.

key phases in the development of the pedipulator has been an intensive study of how nature's walking machines—men and other animals—actually do walk.

In addition to devising new machines, researchers have begun to look to nature for ways to improve present-day machines and vehicles. The first successful airplanes were only roughly modeled after the outline of a bird, and, indeed, in some respects they are quite unbirdlike, since their wings do not flap, and they use propellers or jets as a power source. But when flight designers finally did get around to looking at nature's flying machines—birds and insects— they discovered that bionics could have provided them with some useful shortcuts. Wing flaps and slots to improve the patterns of air flow had been incorporated into bird feather designs millions of years before human inventors thought of them. The marvelous skeleton of a bird, superbly braced for strength yet incredibly light, is the envy of any airplane builder. And birds are far more efficient than any man-made aircraft. The wings of birds soon provided new ideas for airplane wing designs. Now flight engineers are putting birds and insects through wind tunnel tests and building working models of, for example, beetles' wings, to find out just why they are so efficient and whether more of nature's secrets can be adapted to man's uses.

The world of the sea, too, is providing a fertile field for man's inventors to study. Squids and octopuses and even scallops were masters of jet propulsion long before the idea ever occurred to human designers. The gas-filled swim bladders of fish, which are adjusted automatically, provide an ideal device for raising and lowering these "underwater vessels" to any depth desired. Through long ages of adaptation, fish and other sea creatures have developed a streamlined shape that is best suited for slipping through the water with a minimum of slowing drag. Indeed, a new blunt-nosed design for navy submarines has been copied from the highly efficient whale shape.

The study of how whales and dolphins move through the water brought new surprises. Dolphins have been clocked at more than twenty miles an hour. This does not sound very fast; but when scientists calculated the amount

*The bottlenose dolphin can swim rapidly through the water because of
its special skin.*

of power that would be necessary to produce such speeds,
they discovered that it was simply impossible for dolphins
to produce so much power. The same was true for whales.
First the scientists thought that they had made some mistakes in their calculations. But when they checked and re-
checked their figures, they kept getting the same answers.
Finally part of the mystery was solved. Their calculations
were based upon a false assumption: they had used the
rigid hull of a ship as their model. And the movement of
ships through water is slowed down by turbulence—a rough
swirling of the water. When a streamlined object moves
slowly through water or air, the fluid moves easily past it
in smooth layers. This is called laminar flow. But if the

object moves very rapidly, or if it has bumps or sharp edges that break up the layers, turbulence results. New calculations showed that if the dolphins and whales were somehow able to cut down turbulence and achieve laminar flow, then they would have quite enough power to swim at the speeds they do.

One mystery was solved, but an even greater mystery remained: how were dolphins and whales able to achieve laminar flow? This was a problem on which ship designers and airplane manufacturers had been working for many years, and although they had found some ingenious answers, none were really very satisfactory. Perhaps nature again had some ideas that man could use. Max Kramer, a German engineer, had studied the problems of turbulence

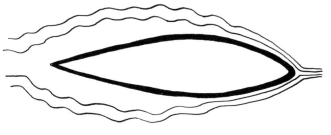

TURBULENT FLOW

LAMINAR FLOW

An object can move much more rapidly through the water if the flow past it is smooth.

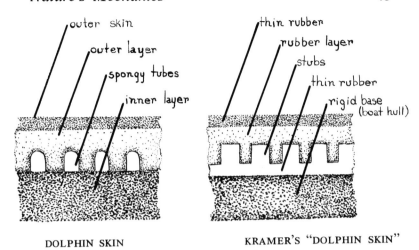

DOLPHIN SKIN   KRAMER'S "DOLPHIN SKIN"

Covering the hull of a boat with artificial "dolphin skin" makes it much faster.

before the Second World War. After the war he came to the United States to work; on the ocean voyage he watched dolphins playing about the ship and became interested in them. Later he examined samples of dolphin skin under a microscope and found that it has a layered structure, with a water-filled, spongy material between the outer and inner layers. As the dolphin moves through the water, whenever a bit of turbulence begins to form, this spongy substance can change its shape and help to smooth out the flow. Kramer devised a rubber skin for boat hulls, modeled after the dolphin skin. When samples were tested on fast-moving boats, it was found that they actually did reduce turbulence, by fifty per cent or more. This dolphinlike skin can also be used to help liquids flow more smoothly through pipelines. The design may even be used someday on the outside of airplanes, to help them to fly more smoothly and rapidly through the air.

Bioluminescence:
Living Lights

The most efficient lights in the world are "living lights"—
the glow produced by living creatures. Such lights can be
found in the depths of the sea, shimmering in the surface
waters, sparking the summer evenings with flashes of brightness, and filling dark caves with an eerie glow.

Scientists are actively studying this phenomenon, which
they call bioluminescence. If man can master the secrets
of bioluminescence, he may be able to make lamps that
work with almost one hundred per cent efficiency, that is,
lamps that give off practically no heat. You have probably
noticed that if you touch an incandescent light bulb that
has been on for a while, it is burning hot. In an incandescent
bulb, the energy of electricity is converted to other forms of
energy: light and heat. It has been estimated that in an incandescent bulb, only about thirty per cent of the electrical
energy is converted to light, while the other seventy per

cent is given off as heat. Yet it is the light we are interested in, and the heat that a light bulb gives off is therefore wasted energy. Indeed, people who have to work under very bright lights—such as in the filming of movies and television shows—find them quite uncomfortable because they are almost unbearably hot. Fluorescent lamps are a bit more efficient, but how much better it would be if we could make lights that give off no heat at all!

Bioluminescence has been found in an enormous variety

Some jellyfish glow in the dark.

of living creatures, from microscopic bacteria and algae to animals such as jellyfish, worms, shrimps, clams, squids, insects, and fishes. Stale meat or fish may take on an eerie glow as bioluminescent bacteria grow and multiply on it. The movement of a passing ship may create a dazzling display of flashing lights in the surface waters of the ocean. In this case the sparkling show is caused by the bioluminescence of dinoflagellates, microscopic light-producing algae that float in the surface waters.

In the depths of the sea, fish cruise about, their way lighted by living lanterns. Other deep-sea fish are marked by rows of luminescent spots like the portholes of an ocean liner. The angler fish dangles a light in front of its nose on a long "fishing pole." The light is used as bait—for if a smaller fish swims up to investigate it, the sharp-toothed angler fish snaps it in. Deep-sea squids do not carry a light with them, but they use bioluminescence in very much the same way that their shallow-water relatives use a black ink. The deep-sea squid can suddenly shoot out a cloud of brightness to dazzle the eyes of its prey or enemies.

The fireflies that flash through the air on summer evenings actually are not flies at all; they are beetles. They can turn the lights in their abdomens on and off, and they usually do so in a very regular rhythm. Fireflies use their flashing lights as mating signals: a male flying through the air blinks on and off in the special pattern for his kind, and he watches the ground below for an answering signal from a female. Then, like a landing airplane, he is guided in to meet her, and they mate. In some parts of Asia, fireflies gather on trees in swarms of thousands and all flash on and off in perfect rhythm.

The larvae of fireflies—young forms without wings—also produce living lights. Indeed, the glowworms that are found in various countries are actually not worms at all, but rather

Some of nature's living lights: (clockwise) the female glow worm, the "railroad worm," and the South American firefly.

the larvae of beetles or flies, or female beetles that never grow wings. One of the strangest of these glowworms is the railroad worm of South America. This beetle larva has a pair of red lights on its head and a row of green lights along each side. If air is blown on the creature, its "headlights" will light up, and if it is shaken, its green side lights will glow.

The lights produced by all these creatures are "cold lights" —they are produced by a complete conversion of chemical energy to light energy, with no wasted heat at all. Scientists have been studying bioluminescent organisms for many years.

trying to find out just how these cold lights work and how the process can be adapted for man's use.

The first progress in bioluminescence research was made about three centuries ago by the great English scientist Robert Boyle. Boyle conducted many experiments on the nature of gases, and he developed an air pump that was a great improvement over those that had been used before. He also became interested in growing luminous bacteria. These creatures are microscopic, but they grow in such enormous numbers that jars of them could be used to light up a room. When Boyle tried pumping the air out of a jar in which luminous bacteria were growing, their light went out. As soon as air was let back into the jar, the glow came on again. Thus Boyle established that air is necessary for the glow of luminous bacteria. (Later, when the element oxygen was discovered, it was found that it is this part of air that is essential for bioluminescence.)

Another important discovery about how bioluminescence works was made in the late nineteenth century by a French scientist, Raphael Dubois. Dubois did his work on luminous clams, which live in holes that they bore in soft rocks near the edge of the Mediterranean Sea. In 1887 he discovered that two kinds of chemicals in the clams were responsible for their living light. One of the chemicals was able to combine with the oxygen of the air, that is, to become oxidized. Dubois named it luciferin, which means "light-bearer." But luciferin could be oxidized only if the other kind of chemical was also present. Dubois named the second type luciferase (the *ase* ending is regularly used for enzymes—chemicals found in living organisms that make other chemicals react).

In the years that followed, luciferin and luciferase were found in many other bioluminescent creatures, from fish to fireflies. It was discovered that the deep-sea squids send out luciferin and luciferase, which mix in the water to form clouds of brightness. The luciferin and luciferase from a tiny clamlike creature called Cypridina will produce a glow when they are moistened, even if they are taken from a dried powder that has been kept for more than twenty years. In fact, the Japanese soldiers used Cypridina powder instead of flashlights during the Second World War. If a soldier wanted to look at a message or a map while he was out on a patrol at night, he moistened some Cypridina powder in the palm of his hand and used its soft glow to read by.

But it seems that different kinds of organisms produce different kinds of luciferin and luciferase. For example, if luciferin from Cypridina is mixed with luciferase from a firefly, nothing will happen. And luciferase from luminous bacteria will not cause luciferin from either Cypridina or fireflies to glow. In each case there is a chemical, a luciferin, that is oxidized, and a second chemical, a luciferase, that makes the reaction take place. But the particular chemicals used by different kinds of organisms are quite different.

Some of the most important modern research on biolumi- nescence has taken place at Johns Hopkins University in Maryland under the leadership of Dr. William D. McElroy. McElroy began his studies of the reaction of luciferin and luciferase in the early 1940s, using fireflies as the source of the material. He and the other scientists of the group dis- covered that another ingredient is needed for the biolumi- nescent reaction—a chemical called ATP, which is used as a source of energy in living things. ATP is not a very com- plicated chemical, in comparison with many other chemi- cals found in living organisms, and it can be manufactured in large quantities. Indeed, the ATP manufacturers now use the luciferin-luciferase reaction to test the purity of their product. The Johns Hopkins group has also succeeded in making luciferin in the laboratory. Research goes on, and perhaps one day wall-sized panels powered by biolumi- nescencelike reactions will bring cool brightness to our homes, schools, and offices.

Bioelectricity: Living Generators

Our modern age is an age of electricity. We are so used to our electric lights, radios and television sets and telephones, toasters and vacuum cleaners, electric trains and elevators, that we find it hard to imagine what life would be like without them. When there is a power failure, people grope about by flickering candlelight, cars hesitate in the streets because there are no traffic lights to guide them, and food spoils in silent refrigerators.

Yet man began to understand how electricity works only a little more than two centuries ago. Nature has apparently been experimenting in this field for millions of years. Scientists are discovering more and more that the living world may hold many interesting secrets of electricity that could benefit mankind.

All living cells send out tiny pulses of electricity. Muscle and nerve cells show particularly high electrical activity. As the heart beats, it sends out pulses of electricity that can be measured and recorded at the surface of the body. When these pulses are recorded, they form an electrocardiogram, which a doctor can study to determine how well the heart is working. The brain, too, sends out brain waves of electricity, which can be recorded in an electroencephalogram. It has been found that even plants generate electric fields and currents as they live and grow. The electric currents generated by most living cells are extremely small—often so small that our most sensitive instruments are needed to record them. But in some animals, certain muscle cells have become so specialized as electrical generators that they do not work as muscle cells at all. When large numbers of these cells are linked together, the effects can be astonishing.

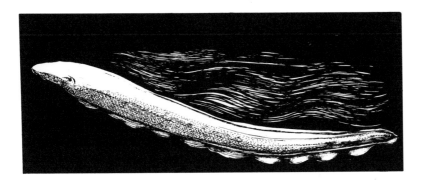

The electric eel.

The electric eel, *Electrophorus electricus,* which lives in the Amazon and other rivers of South America, is an amazing living storage battery. It can send a jolt of as much as 800 volts of electricity through the water in which it lives! (Our electric house current is only 120 volts.) As many as four fifths of all the cells in the electric eel's body are specialized for generating electricity, and the size of the shock it can deliver corresponds roughly to the length of its body. (These slender fish can grow to a length of nine feet or more.) It has been calculated that the electric eel's power output, per gram of its weight, is about a hundred times as great as that of the lead storage batteries used in automobiles.

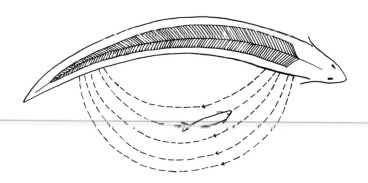

The electric eel sends a current of electricity out into the water.

The electric eel uses its enormous electrical discharges to catch its prey. The bodies of fish and other living creatures conduct electricity better than the water in which they live; when the electric eel sends out pulses of electricity, other fishes in the neighborhood attract them like lightning rods. They are stunned or even killed by the shock, and then the eel can easily gobble them down.

Scientists have found that a special control center in the electric eel's brain triggers its discharges. The eel can control not only the frequency or the rapidity with which one discharge follows another, but also the size of the shock. Indeed, the electric eel has been found to generate two other kinds of electrical activity, at a much lower voltage. It seems to use one type as a sort of electrical location system, with which it senses the presence of other living creatures by the way they change the electric field that the eel sets up in the water. Researchers are not yet sure about the use of the other type, but they think it may act as a sort of electric lure for the eel's prey. Fishermen have discovered that they can attract tuna and certain other fish by sending out an electric current of a particular frequency and strength. And the second type of low-voltage electric shock that the electric eel sends out is very similar to the currents that human fishermen have learned to use to catch more fish.

The electric eel is only one of many types of fish that use electricity in their daily lives. Some live in salt waters, while others live in the fresh waters of rivers and streams; the electrical activity of these fishes is generally adapted to take advantage of the kind of watery world in which they live. Salt water, for example, conducts electricity better than fresh water, while swift, swirling waters tend to break up the pattern of electric fields, so that very fast pulses are needed to bring the fish any useful information.

The electric catfish of Africa is much smaller than the electric eel, but it can generate shocks of up to 350 volts. The electric ray, which lives in the North Atlantic, was used by the ancient Romans to treat various diseases, including some forms of mental illness. In a way this was similar to the electroshock therapy that is used by some psychiatrists to treat mental illness today.

In addition to the fish that generate enormous electric shocks, there are many types that can produce only a weak electrical activity, which they use in electrical location systems. One of these electric fishes, *Gymnarchus niloticus,* has been studied by Hans Lissmann, a zoologist from Cambridge University. *Gymnarchus,* which lives in the muddy waters of the Nile and other African rivers, is a slender fish with a long, rippling fin on the upper surface of its back. It swims very peculiarly: it does not undulate back and forth as most fish do, but holds its body stiff and straight as a broomstick, swimming and steering by movements of its fin. It has an electric organ that generates very weak pulses of electricity. Indeed, scientists thought at first that it was a pseudoelectric organ, because they believed that it did not have any use at all.

Lissmann found that he could catch *Gymnarchus* with a magnet! Floating along an African river in a rowboat, he caught sight of one of these fish swimming in the water. He held a strong horseshoe magnet just above the surface of the water, and the fish came swimming up to it. Wherever the zoologist moved the magnet, the fish followed, keeping its head just below the magnet. It would even follow a hard rubber comb to which Lissmann had given an electric charge by running it rapidly through his hair.

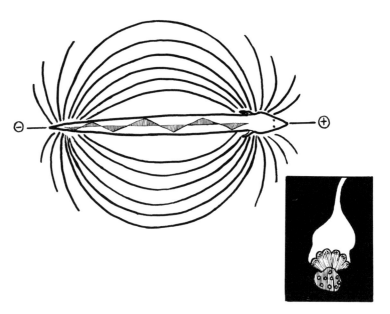

GYMNARCHUS *sends weak electric currents out into the water and senses them with special electric sense organs.*

Lissmann caught a number of *Gymnarchus* specimens and took them home to his laboratory to study. He found that the fish's electric organ sends out pulses of electricity from the region of its tail. An electric field is set up in the water, very much like the field around a bar magnet. If any object is in the water nearby, it will change the pattern of this field, and then *Gymnarchus* will be able to tell not only where the object is, but also how large it is and how it is shaped. The fish can even tell whether the object is living or not—for living things tend to conduct electricity better than plain water, while nonliving things, such as a rock or a dead log, are generally poor conductors. Depending on whether an object is a good conductor or not, it will change the electric field in quite different ways. Thus, in spite of its poor eyesight and the muddy waters, *Gymnarchus* can find and catch its prey quite effectively.

The electric world of *Gymnarchus* and the other electric fishes is a very difficult one for us to imagine. For we do not have any senses for perceiving electricity. Even if we get a powerful shock from touching a live wire or open electrical outlet, we are not really sensing the electricity itself, but rather its effects on our body.

Gymnarchus and the other electric fishes do have special sense organs for perceiving electricity. Lissmann found that their skin is unusually thick, made up of layers of platelike cells. This skin provides a fine natural insulation, but scattered among the tiny plates are small openings or pores. These pores are especially numerous around the head, and each leads into a tube filled with a jellylike substance that is a good conductor of electricity. The jelly tends to focus electric currents like a lens, and at the bottom of each pore is a group of sense cells that are linked by nerves to the brain. The area of *Gymnarchus'* brain that receives and analyzes the information from its electric sense organs is very large

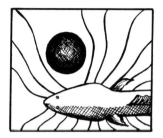

The pattern formed in the water by GYMNARCHUS'
electric currents is changed by the presence of a
poor conductor (left) or a good conductor (right).

and well developed, just as the area for analyzing sound
information is the best developed in the bat's brain. Lissmann's observations of how *Gymnarchus* uses its electric currents explain why the fish holds its body so stiff when it
swims: if it were in constant movement, the pattern of the
electric field would be constantly changing, and *Gymnarchus*
could not get any meaningful information from it.

The knife-fishes that live in muddy rivers of South America use an electrical location system very similar to that of
Gymnarchus. These fish also keep their bodies stiff when they
swim, moving by undulations of a long, ribbonlike fin at the
underside of their bodies. These electric fish hunt at night,
when the larger predators are asleep. Then, as the morning
light begins to filter through the water, the knife-fish seek
shelter among the rocks and weeds on the river bottom close
to the shore. Large numbers may hide there together, all
sending out their pulses of electricity even as they sleep.
They use their weak eyes only to tell the difference between
night and day.

Gymnarchus generally sends out its electrical pulses at a
rate of about three hundred per second. But what happens
when two of these fish pass close by one another? The two
electrical fields interfere with one another, and each fish has

difficulty sorting out the information from its own signals. Scientists at the University of Tokyo have discovered that *Gymnarchus* has solved this problem: when the electric fields of two of these fish begin to interfere, they stop transmitting for a moment. Then each shifts its frequency slightly, so that they are soon sending out electrical pulses at different rates. Now each fish can tell which signals are its own.

The electrical pulses of our telephones and telegraphs are modulated, changed in complex ways so that they can carry a wealth of information. Experiments with *Gymnarchus* indicate that its electrical pulses are smoothed out and do not carry information in this way. But it has been found that another kind of weakly electric fish, the elephant-nose fish (*Mormyrus*) of Africa, does use electrical signals for communication, in addition to its electrical location system. Some elephant-nose fish live in large schools and use electrical signals to keep their schools together. Other species prefer to live alone, and they use electrical signals to mark off the boundaries of their territories. A zoologist from West Germany's Tübingen University, Franz Möhres, witnessed many "electric duels" between elephant-nose fish. Each fish constantly gives off its own electrical pulses. If one strays over the boundary line of another's territory, he will begin to feel the electric field from the owner of the territory more and more strongly. The owner will know from the presence

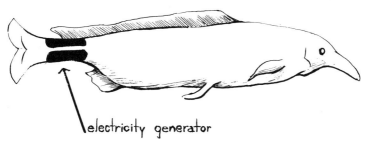

electricity generator

The elephant-nose fish is another electric fish.

of a strange electric field that there is a trespasser in his territory. Each fish will now build up his electric discharges in strength and frequency. As the argument rages, very much like the furious song contests of songbirds, the intruding fish will usually back away, and the discharges will quiet down. But if he persists, the electrical argument will eventually turn into a real fight, with the two fish ramming and biting each other until one is the winner.

It was studies of animal electricity two centuries ago that helped to establish the nature of electric current and resulted in the invention of the electrochemical battery. Today's scientists hope that further studies of nature's living generators will reveal new secrets that can be used in man's inventions.

One of the most exciting ways in which studies of bioelectricity are already bringing benefits to man are in applications to aid the human body itself. Thousands of people alive today would have died years ago if it were not for small electronic devices, called cardiac pacemakers, implanted inside their bodies. The body normally has a pacemaker of its own: a small structure that sends signals to the heart muscle and controls the rate of its beating. But sometimes the body's pacemaker fails. Until electronic substitutes were invented, such failure meant certain death. Physicians and engineers have worked together to make electronic pacemakers smaller and more efficient, and to improve the batteries that power them so that they do not have to be replaced frequently (for replacement means an operation). Now they are working to devise pacemakers that can be powered by the body's own electricity, or by electricity generated in special crystals by the contractions of the heart itself.

The invention of the cardiac pacemaker is a typical example of the fruitful co-operation between doctors and engineers in the growing new field of medical electronics.

This co-operation has also produced artificial limbs that can be powered by the body's own electricity. An amputee with such an artificial hand merely thinks about what he wants the hand to do, just as he would if he still had his own hand, and electrical messages flash along the muscles and nerves of his arm. They are linked to an electronic device in the

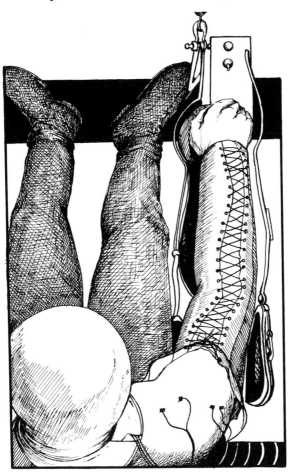

An electronic muscle-power amplifier helps an astronaut to move even under a heavy gravity load during takeoff.

artificial hand, the signals are amplified, and the mechanical fingers of the hand perform the task. Similar devices are also helping to bypass dead nerve pathways in paralyzed limbs, to enable the patients to move them again. Devices to amplify muscle signals will also have important uses in the exploration of space. As a spaceship accelerates during take-off, an astronaut's body is subjected to such enormous stresses of gravity that even to move a lever may require tremendous strength. Electronic amplifiers can use the muscles' own signals to give the added boost that is needed.

One of the most intriguing of the experiments with bio-electricity is a series of studies sponsored by the U.S. Navy. Researchers are working on ways to link man with machinery, so that electrical messages from the brain can control machines. In one model that has already been built, a man can actually turn a light on and off just by thinking about it!

Thinking Machines

One of the favorite themes in science fiction is the robot. This mechanical man can do nearly everything a real human can do. But it can work under conditions that would not be safe for men, or perform great feats of strength, or have other valuable special abilities. We have already seen a number of ways in which bionic studies may someday aid scientists and engineers to build robots: studies of the senses, to gain information about the environment; studies of the mechanics of nature, to help in building machines that can move about like men; studies of bioelectricity, which may provide keys to co-ordination and control. But can we ever build a machine that can really think?

What about electronic computers? Are they thinking machines?

Scientists and engineers have already designed and built electronic computers that are capable of amazing feats. They can store millions of bits of information, in a memory that never grows faint or fuzzy, and can find and use any one of these pieces of information in an instant. They can do millions of calculations in a second and can solve complicated problems that would take many lifetimes of work for human mathematicians. But most of these computers are just what their name implies—computing machines. They can add and subtract and do other calculations; they can do them far faster than we can; but they cannot think and learn as humans do.

Researchers are now trying to build machines that can truly think and learn. They are using a number of different approaches. Some are studying the brain and the nervous system, to find out how they work. Some are studying how humans and other animals remember and learn. Some are trying to build simple electronic models of nerve cells and learning machines.

When a scientist builds an electronic model of a nerve cell, or neuron, he does not try merely to copy its structure. Instead, he studies what a neuron does and then tries to put together electronic components to do the same things.

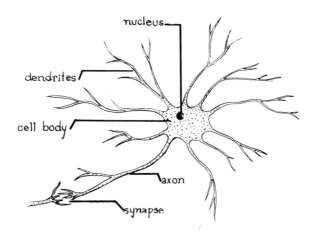

A typical nerve cell.

When a neuron receives a suitable message or stimulus, it "fires"—it carries an electrical message along its length and eventually passes it on to another neuron. The stimulus must be of the proper strength for the neuron to fire; if it is too weak, the message will not be carried along. After the neuron has fired, it requires a certain time, perhaps a split second, to recover; until it has recovered, it cannot fire again, even if a new stimulus is applied. Some stimuli work in a different way—they inhibit the neuron, or keep it from firing.

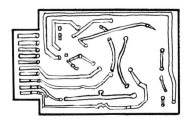 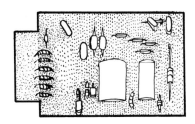

Cross section of an artificial nerve cell; its manner of working is modeled after a nerve cell, but it does not look at all like one.

The bionics specialist constructing a model neuron must take all these things into account. A number of different kinds of electronic model neurons, with names such as "neuromime," "neuristor," and "artron," have been built, and some of them are quite good models of what a neuron does.

But a single neuron, which is either *on* or *off,* is not very useful. Our brains are made up of millions of neurons, interconnected in a fantastic number of complicated networks. When researchers tried hooking up their artificial neurons into networks, they achieved some interesting results. The model of the frog's eye and its links to the brain, which is helping in the development of electronic guidance systems, was constructed completely from electronic circuits. And experimenters have already built some interesting learning machines that really learn, rather than merely compute.

A very simple learning machine called Learm was first demonstrated in 1954. It was shaped like a worm, and it received information through three simple switch inputs in its head, one in the center and one on each side. Learm was trained in a T-shaped maze, very much like the mazes that are used to train flatworms and earthworms. It moved up the long arm of the T, and when it reached the branching point, it bumped its central input switch, causing it to turn either to the left or to the right. At first Learm was just as likely to choose either one. But then an object was placed in one arm of the T. If Learm chose that side, it got a "reward"—the switch on that side of its head was activated, and a charge was placed on its memory storage on that side. If Learm received a reward on the right side of the T-maze, it tended to turn that way again the next time. The more rewards it received, the more likely it was to turn to the right, until it could make the "correct" choice each time, without any mistakes. But then if the rewards were stopped, Learm gradually forgot its lessons and began to choose either side again.

Scientists were encouraged by how similar the behavior of this simple machine was to the behavior of a real worm in the same kind of maze. They went on to build more complicated learning machines. Some can learn to recognize patterns, like the letters of the alphabet or pictures of people's faces. They can be taught to recognize only parts of these patterns, such as the top of a person's hairdo or his mouth and chin. This is what a learning machine in London, the UCLM II, learned to do. But the job of teaching it turned out to be so boring that the researchers finally assigned it to a special teaching machine, which patiently showed the same patterns to UCLM II over and over again and corrected it every time it made a mistake.

Machines have also been taught to play games, such as ticktacktoe, checkers, and chess. Playing these games successfully requires thinking ahead, to figure out what the other player may do, and what choices will be left in each possible case. One computer programmed at IBM Research Laboratories beat a human checkers champion; some other computers can play very good chess against human players. Another computer has been designed to use its experience in learning the rules of one game to learn other games more easily.

Some computers can be programed to play games like checkers.

Meanwhile, advances in solid-state physics are making it possible to build complicated electronic circuits on tiny crystal chips so small that they have to be assembled under a microscope. With these new advances, electronic engineers are gaining the ability to build more and more compact and complicated computers, with a number of interconnections that may one day rival those of the human brain itself. As these engineers co-operate with biologists who are learning more and more about the secrets of the brain, perhaps some-day soon man will be able to build machines that can truly think.

Glossary

---

amplifier—a device for increasing power (or wound, electrical pulses, etc.)

ATP— the abbreviation for adenosine triphosphate, one of the most common chemicals used by living organisms to store energy

bioluminescence—the production of light by living organisms, without by-production of heat

bionics— the study of systems in living creatures and their applications for the improvement of man-made systems

cardiac pacemaker—an electronic device that regulates the rate of the heartbeat in persons whose own pacemakers do not work properly

circadian rhythm— a regular cycle in the life and activities of an organism, which repeats itself regularly in a period of about twenty-four hours

collagen—a protein substance found in skin and other living materials; collagen fibers have been used in artificial muscles

compound eye—an eye consisting of numerous tiny lenses, each of which contributes a part to the complete picture of the environment; found in insects and some other animals

electrocardiogram—a recording of the electrical activity of the heart

electroencephalogram—a recording of the electrical activity of the brain

enzyme—a chemical produced by a living organism that aids others chemicals to react

gas chromatograph—an instrument in which mixtures of gases and vapors are separated as they are carried along by a stream of gas

jet propulsion—a means of propelling an object forward through the reaction to the backward push of a stream ("jet") of liquid or compressed gas

laminar flow—smooth flow of a fluid in layers past a moving object

larva—immature form of an insect, often roughly worm-shaped

lens—a device for focusing light rays or other forms of radiation

luciferase—an enzyme that causes luciferin to react with oxygen

luciferin—a chemical that combines with oxygen to produce bioluminescence

manipulator—a mechanical device for picking up and handling objects in a manner similar to the operation of the human hand

migration—movement of a group of animals of the same species to a new area because of a change in season, in search of a new food supply, etc.; observed in birds, fishes, insects, and various other types of animals

neuron—a nerve cell

ommatidium—one of the tiny lenses in a compound eye

pedipulator—a "walking machine" on legs

photocell—an electronic device that is sensitive to light and transmits electrical signals when it is exposed to light

pit organ—heat-sensitive organ in the head of a rattlesnake

radar—location system based on the analysis of reflected radio waves

retina—the light-sensitive layer at the back of the eyeball

sex attractant—a chemical produced by an animal of one sex, which attracts members of the opposite sex; usually each species produces its own specific chemical or chemicals

sonar—sound-location system based on the analysis of sound waves reflected from solid objects

turbulence—rough swirling of water or other fluid as it flows past an uneven surface

ultrasound—sound waves so high-pitched that human ears cannot detect them

Index